THE
OUTDOOR
MUSEUM

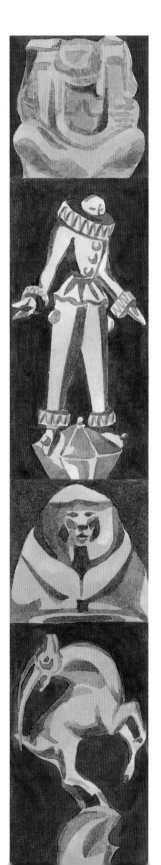

THE OUTDOOR MUSEUM

THE MAGIC OF MICHIGAN'S MARSHALL M. FREDERICKS

BY
MARCY HELLER FISHER

ILLUSTRATED BY
CHRISTINE COLLINS WOOMER

WAYNE STATE UNIVERSITY PRESS
DETROIT

Great Lakes Books

A complete listing of the books in this series can be found at the back of this volume.

Philip P. Mason, Editor

Dr. Charles K. Hyde, Associate Editor

Department of History, Wayne State University

Department of History, Wayne State University

Library of Congress Cataloging-in-Publication Data

Fisher, Marcy Heller, 1953-
   The outdoor museum : the magic of Michigan's Marshall M. Fredericks / by Marcy Heller Fisher ;
illustrated by Christine Collins Woomer.
      p. cm. — (Great Lakes books)
   Summary: Because she is fascinated by a statue she sees while skating, Abby and her mother spend a
day looking at the sculptures of Marshall Fredericks around the city of Detroit, Michigan. Includes
information about the sculptor, his work and the sculptural process, as well as a list of sculptures to be
seen throughout Michigan and in other Great Lakes states.
   ISBN 0-8143-2932-2 (alk. paper) — ISBN 0-8143-2969-1 (pbk. : alk. paper)
   1. Fredericks, Marshall M., 1908-1998—Juvenile fiction. [1. Fredericks, Marshall M., 1908-1998—
Fiction. 2. Sculpture—Fiction. 3. Detroit (Mich.)—Fiction.] I. Woomer, Christine Collins, ill. II.
Title. III. Series.
   PZ7.F5344 Ou 2001
   [Fic]—dc21

                                                                              00-011675

PERMISSIONS AND CREDITS

Photograph of Marshall M. Fredericks in his studio, by Molly Barth, courtesy of Marshall M. Fredericks Studio

Photograph of Marshall Fredericks carving of *Victory Eagle*, courtesy of Marshall M. Fredericks Studio

Photograph of Marshall Fredericks building a plaster model, courtesy of Marshall M. Fredericks Studio

Photograph of *The Boy and Bear* on opening day at Northland Center, courtesy of Joanne K. Lichtenstein
Viviano, reprinted by Paul Cooney, and used with the permission of Northland Center

Grateful acknowledgment is made to the Marshall M. Fredericks Sculpture Museum at Saginaw
Valley State University and to the Frederik Meijer Gardens and Sculpture Park in Grand Rapids
for the generous support of the publication of this volume.

I love people, for I have learned through so many experiences, both happy and sad, how beautiful and wonderful they can be; therefore I want more than anything in the world to do sculpture which will have real meaning for other people, many people, and might in some way encourage, inspire, or give them happiness.

—Marshall Fredericks, *Credo*

To Rob, Seth, Benjamin,
Gabriel, and Abigail

CONTENTS

PREFACE

Marshall Maynard Fredericks, one of America's leading twentieth-century figurative sculptors, died in 1998 at the age of ninety, after having spent more than sixty years living and working in Michigan. His home on Quarton Lake in Birmingham and his studio in Royal Oak have since been sold. His private garden, which showcased many of his sculptures, has been dismantled. Yet Fredericks's legacy—hundreds of sculptures in Michigan—can be uncovered on walking tours in downtown Detroit, Royal Oak, and Birmingham, at the Detroit Zoo, Cranbrook Educational Community in Bloomfield Hills, and the University of Michigan campus in Ann Arbor. Banks, churches, libraries, and city centers all over the state are enhanced by Fredericks's art. His sculptures at Interlochen and Indian River, in northern lower Michigan, are tourist destinations, as is the Marshall M. Fredericks Sculpture Museum at Saginaw Valley State University. Dedicated to displaying hundreds of Fredericks's original plaster models, and preserving photographs, sketches, and objects related to his life's work, this museum's remarkable collection also includes numerous bronze casts in its sculpture garden and on the grounds of the campus. More of his bronze sculptures can be seen while exploring the Frederik Meijer Gardens and Sculpture Park in Grand Rapids, owned by the West Michigan Horticultural Society. Amidst an extraordinary collection by several twentieth-century artists, dozens of Marshall Fredericks sculptures are scattered over 118 acres of meticulously tended botanical

gardens as well as inside the Lena Meijer Conservatory.

Readers can duplicate Abby's discoveries of these works, following the trajectory she takes in this story or traveling around Michigan and other Great Lakes states. *The Outdoor Museum* includes a selected list of Fredericks's sculptures in the region as well as album pages to personalize this book.

ACKNOWLEDGMENTS

When I first asked him if I could write a book about his work, Marshall Fredericks, the most modest of gentlemen, was hesitant. However, when I told him it would be for children, he was delighted. Shortly before he died, Mr. Fredericks and his wife opened their home, hearts, and garden to me, while he and his assistant, Molly Barth, graciously allowed me access to his studio. I owe them my gratitude and thanks.

I could not tell this story without following the same path as in the book. My traveling companion Rob, who endured the bumps and wrong turns with nothing but encouragement, along with our backseat boosters—Seth, Benjamin, Gabriel, and Abigail—made that journey even more enjoyable. You know how much I love and appreciate you. Special thanks go to my sister Barbara Heller for her staunch encouragement and midnight editing; to Suki Fredericks, who supported my endless requests and championed this book; and to Pam Pangborn and Scott Slocum from the Marshall Fredericks Studio, who, along with Molly Barth, painstakingly searched archives and documents for me. My mother introduced me to Marshall Fredericks's works and inspired me as a child. What she imparted to me, I hope to convey to the next generation.

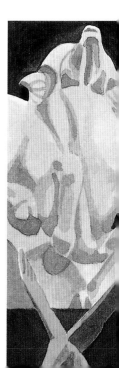

A national treasure, a real living and breathing hero, lived in the neighborhood. Abby had never met him, but she'd skated by his house and been captivated by his sculptures. She found them all around town—bronze pterodactyls, soaring humans, bears, lions, rams and clowns—dotting the landscape and inspiring everyone who happened upon them. Each sculpture seemed to beckon her: come soar with me, sit on my lap, or ride on my back. Abby was touched by this magic, as you will be too.

The Secret of Quarton Lake

Abby dug her skates into the ice, tilting her head to check her progress. A patch of green in the otherwise all-white landscape caught her eye. She twirled around for a second glance and continued gliding across the lake, aiming toward the fenced yard where mystery beckoned.

"Mom, come over here and look!" Abby called as she passed.

"I don't have skates on. What do you want me to see?" her mother replied from the bank.

"Mom, there's something behind those trees. Look across the lake. Can you see those greenish-colored shapes that look like animals?" Abby stopped and pointed.

"Those are sculptures, honey. That's the home of Marshall Fredericks. He's been my favorite sculptor since I was a child. He must have some of his sculptures in his garden."

"Can we go see them?" Abby asked, as she skated back toward her mom.

"No, honey, that's his home, but you see one of his sculptures every day. Just outside the front entrance of Quarton School. . . ."

"The bears?" Abby interrupted.

"Yes, the *Two Bears* are by Marshall Fredericks. When you go back to school on Monday, why don't you take another look at them?"

"No, Mom, I'm done skating. Could we please go see them now?"

Unlacing her skates, Abby looked back across the lake and pondered her new discovery. I love coming here, she thought, fishing with Grandpa in the summer, feeding geese in the fall, and especially skating in the winter, but I never noticed those sculptures before. As she pulled her boots up, she became even more excited. Wait 'til I tell Kim the secret of Quarton Lake, she thought excitedly.

That's how it was with Abby and her friends: a secret wasn't special unless it could be shared.

With her skates swung over her shoulders, Abby helped pull her mom off the embankment and they started out over the bridge. "It's close, let's just walk there," her mother suggested.

Abby ran up to the school's entrance. "Look Mom, here are the bears. But they're brown, not that greenish color I saw at Quarton Lake." Abby rattled on as she put down her skates and used her gloved hand to touch one of the bears' bellies. "They're cold and hard, but they look so warm and friendly."

"This is cast in bronze, Abby," her mom explained. "There are different finishes on bronze sculptures. This sculpture has a brown-colored patina [pa-teen-a]. The sea-green hue you saw at the lake is called verdigris [ver-duh-gree]."

"Look," Abby said, "the plaque says it's called *Two Bears, Friends, Big and Small*, but everyone at school just calls them *The Bears*. They're our school mascots. I think Mr. Fredericks must like children."

"I think you're right. In fact I believe there are five Fredericks children, and they all went to your school. That's one of the reasons your school has a Marshall Fredericks sculpture."

Together, they reached out and touched the bears' heads, tracing the lines of the animals' friendly faces with their gloved hands.

Abby's mother stepped back to contemplate the sculpture. "You know, even though this sculpture is meant for children, it still inspires me. Remember I told you that Marshall Fredericks was my favorite sculptor when I was a child?" Abby looked up at her mother and nodded. "When I was growing up in Detroit, I always thought that Marshall Fredericks was in charge of decorating the city!"

"Mom," Abby interrupted, "how could anyone be in charge of decorating a whole city?"

"Oh, I know it sounds silly now, but as a child, whenever I went somewhere special with your grandma and grandpa, there always seemed to be a Marshall Fredericks sculpture. When we went downtown, I always looked for *The Spirit of Detroit*, or the *Victory Eagle*. In the summer we'd picnic near the *Leaping Gazelle* Fountain on Belle Isle. From the art museum, I could see the Marshall Fredericks reliefs that surround the Rackham Memorial Building next door. On holidays, your grandma and grandpa would take us to the Ford Auditorium for a ballet or concert. The foyer walls were covered with his *Harlequins* and visions of the *Ford Empire*. And at Christmas we'd take a trip to the Ford Rotunda, which always used to be decorated for the holidays; I'd wander around memorizing the Marshall Fredericks reliefs that surrounded the round viewing space, while your grandmother would be 'oohing and aahing' at the holiday decorations and your grandfather would be looking at the new cars!"

"That sounds like fun. Can we go during winter break?" Abby asked.

"No, honey, the Ford Rotunda burned down many years ago. It was one of our favorite places to visit!"

"Where else did you go with Grandma and Grandpa that made you think Marshall Fredericks was decorating the city?" Abby asked.

"Oh, at the zoo Grandma used to tell us to meet her at the 'Marshall Fredericks' in case we became separated—she meant the *Pterodactyls* just outside the Reptile House. Marshall Fredericks even designed the furniture in the old ape exhibit. And when Grandma went shopping at Northland Center, your aunts and I would climb and play on Marshall Fredericks's *The Boy and Bear*. So you see, I didn't know who Marshall Fredericks was, nor where he came from, but it always seemed that every special place we went would have sculptures, and every time I saw a sculpture, your grandma would tell me it was created by Marshall Fredericks. In fact, it really wasn't until your daddy and I moved to Birmingham when you were a baby that I found out Mr. Fredericks was living and working in our neighborhood."

"Mr. Fredericks must be awfully old if he was famous when you were a child!" Abby exclaimed.

"He's probably as old as your grandpa. Yet I've heard that Mr. Fredericks still goes to his studio every day and works on new sculptures. He must be in his late eighties, which means he's been creating his magic for at least sixty years."

"Mom, will you take me to the city to see all those sculptures?" Abby inquired.

"Sure, that sounds like fun. Why don't you invite your friend Kim to join us next Saturday, and we'll make a whole day of it? But right now I want to show you a surprise. Are you too cold to walk to town?"

Birmingham, Michigan, is one of those fast-disappearing American cities where people still enjoy walking to town: to shop, go to the library, or even stroll in the park. Abby knew her mom hated parking in town, so she agreed to walk. As they turned off the main street, Abby guessed where they were heading.

"Are we going to the library?"

"Yes—and look at that," Abby's mom said, as they started toward the Baldwin Library.

Abby watched two little boys walking toward the entrance. They stopped and looked up at a sculpture called *Siberian Ram*. One of the little boys plopped down to get some snow, then tried to feed it to the ram.

"Is that one of his sculptures too? I've seen that a million times, but it's not bronze like the *Two Bears*. It looks like stone. May I get closer so I can touch it?"

"Keep your mittens on if you do. Every time you touch a sculpture, whether it's in limestone like this ram or bronze like the *Two Bears*, you leave fingerprints. The oils from fingerprints cause smudges that collect dirt and damage the sculptures. In summer, this sculpture will be surrounded by flowers to protect it."

Abby and her mother paused to browse at the Baldwin Library. Abby found a book on sculpture but she couldn't find a book about Marshall Fredericks.

"Mom, I thought he was famous. Why aren't there any books about him?"

"Sometimes we take for granted the heroes in our midst. To this day, Mr. Fredericks is still creating. His work isn't done. Maybe you could write about his sculptures and what they mean to you."

Abby thought that was a terrific idea. She loved to write and was entranced by her new discoveries.

"I have one more thing to show you today," Abby's mother said, "and it's just across the street. . . ."

"In the park? Oh, I know just where it is," and she ran toward the middle of Shain Park. Abby looked up at the soaring sculpture in wonderment. "Look, the sign says it's called *Freedom of the Human Spirit*. What does that mean?"

"Well, Abby, art says different things to different people. You don't have to understand art or be an artist to be inspired by it. How does the sculpture make you feel? What does it say to you?"

"I want to think about it," Abby said, suddenly remembering how cold her feet were. "May we please stop for some hot chocolate while I think? I'm freezing."

It had been an adventurous afternoon. Daylight ends early in the winter, so for the moment their exploring was done. Abby and her mother chatted about their discoveries over hot chocolate and cookies at a bakery overlooking the park.

As soon as they got home, Abby ran up to her room to call Kim and tell her about the mysteries she'd seen at the lake. She asked Kim to sleep over Friday night so they could be ready to leave early Saturday morning for their adventure. "And don't forget your camera," she said.

Treasure-Tripping to Detroit

The girls woke early, groggy from having talked and giggled through the night, but excited about their planned mysterious adventure. "We're going on a photo safari, in search of sculptures by Marshall Fredericks," Abby's mom explained, while handing the girls their cameras and a package of film.

"Mom says we'll see a Marshall Fredericks sculpture wherever we look, but I think she's exaggerating," Abby warned.

They took the expressway, and the girls didn't see any sculptures. But as they neared downtown, Mom warned the girls to get their cameras ready. The car passed the former Veterans Memorial Building and Abby's mother pointed out Marshall Fredericks's seven pylons and *Victory Eagle* jutting out from the building's facade.

"Mom, you're going too fast, I missed the picture," Abby complained.

"Don't worry, we'll walk back there in a few minutes. I think we should start our tour at *The Spirit of Detroit*." She parked the car and pointed across the street. Abby and Kim popped out of their seats and stared in awe at *The Spirit*.

"Wow!" the girls cried out in unison. The sculpture was humongous—a man,

as tall as a building, sitting with his legs crossed under him, in that same greenish-colored patina Abby had seen from Quarton Lake. He held a family in his right hand and the world in his left.

"Detroiters love this sculpture so much that it's become the symbol of the city. Just look around." Abby's mom pointed at silhouettes of *The Spirit of Detroit* on information signs, on a police car across the street, and even on the banners decorating Jefferson Avenue. "I believe that Mr. Fredericks didn't even name this sculpture, I think it became known as *The Spirit of Detroit* because the citizens were so moved by it."

"I remember seeing him on TV," Kim said. "He was wearing a huge Red Wings jersey when the Wings won the Stanley Cup."

Abby's mother smiled. "When I was in high school, someone painted giant green footsteps from *The Spirit* to a sculpture of a woman across the street!"

"I don't remember if it was Valentine's Day or St. Patrick's Day, but I do remember all the radio stations and the newspapers having a laugh about it. In those days, we used to call him the "Jolly Green Giant." And later, when Mayor Coleman Young died, *The Spirit* wore a black armband, once again reflecting the mood of the city."

"I love *The Spirit*. It's my favorite sculpture!" Abby exclaimed.

They walked back to the former Veterans Memorial Building and took photos of each other standing by Marshall Fredericks's pylons depicting the history of the city. A huge marble eagle jutted out from the facade of the building. "The V-shape symbolizes both victory and the veterans, in honor of those who were in World War II," Abby's mother explained. "And this last pylon is in honor of the end of World War II."

At the Ford Auditorium, a short distance away and just past Hart Plaza, a sympathetic security guard allowed the girls a peek inside the foyer. The *Harlequins* and *Circus Parades* were difficult to see in the dimmed light of the now-closed auditorium, but Abby thought the metal wall sculptures must have made quite an impression on people when the building was open.

The last stop before leaving downtown was across a bridge to visit Belle Isle, an island park in the middle of the Detroit River. "Did you really picnic here all the time when you were little?" Kim asked. "This island is so beautiful." Abby was thinking the same thing.

Driving around the park, Abby spied the *Leaping Gazelle Fountain*. "That's by Marshall Fredericks, isn't it?" she called happily.

"That's probably his most famous sculpture," Abby's mother answered. She parked the car and the girls climbed out, running toward the frozen fountain. They ran around the perimeter, wiping snow off the heads of the four black granite animals that surrounded the bronze gazelle.

"Can you name the animals?" Abby's mother asked. "I believe they're all native to this island."

"An otter . . . ," replied Kim.

"A rabbit . . . and a. . . ." Abby wasn't sure.

"A hawk and a grouse, I believe," answered Abby's mother.

"I've changed my mind, *this* is my favorite Marshall Fredericks sculpture!"

The Malls

Tired, chilled, and hungry, the girls fell asleep in the car. Abby's mother decided to drive to Eastland Mall so the girls could warm up, have a bite to eat, and see another sculpture. As they entered the mall, she explained that Eastland and Northland were two of the first shopping centers in the country, and that the architect had commissioned Marshall Fredericks sculptures for both of them, especially for children. Kim had caught Abby's excitement and they both ran through the mall looking for their treasure.

"There it is, Abby." Kim called. "That must be *The Lion and Mouse* from *Aesop's Fables*." They came upon a friendly-looking limestone lion lying on his back, staring at a little golden mouse perched on his belly. Unfortunately, the sculpture was surrounded by ropes so the girls couldn't get close to it. A nearby guard explained that vandals had tried to steal the mouse, and the ropes were there to protect the sculpture. This made Abby sad. The girls took turns posing like the lion and making faces at the mouse. Abby's mother captured their frolicking on film.

"I've changed my mind again, Mom. This *definitely* is my favorite sculpture! I like how the stone is carved so the lion has a curly mane. And I love the little golden-colored mouse."

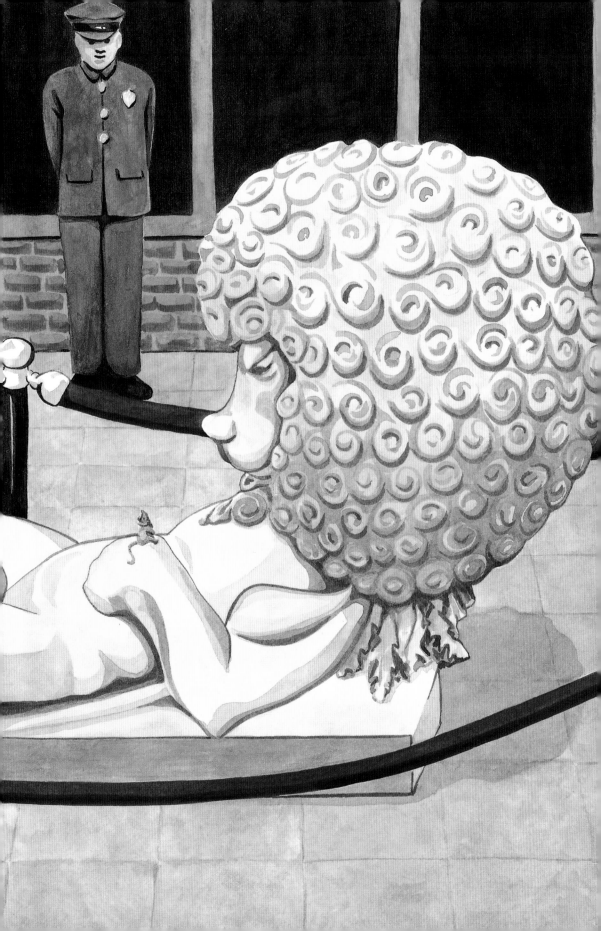

Once again, Abby's mother only smiled. At lunch Kim asked if there were a lot more Marshall Fredericks sculptures around town.

"I think we could spend a few more days just in the Detroit area, but there's only time for one more today. If you girls would like, we could squeeze a few more in next week, but we'd better buy more film."

The last stop for the day was Northland Center. As she drove across town, Abby's mother pulled out an old black and white photograph. "I dug this picture out the other day after you were skating at Quarton Lake. It shows your aunts playing on Marshall Fredericks's *The Boy and Bear* on opening day at Northland Center, more than forty years ago. When I was a little girl, *that* was my favorite sculpture!"

The girls held the photo carefully. The stone sculpture dwarfed the girls in the picture. On the bear's back was a little boy. "I bet that's one of Mr. Fredericks's own kids on the bear's back," Abby said.

The Boy and Bear was easy to find. As the girls ran up to the sculpture, Abby reached up and touched the bear's face. "Mom, I like this sculpture best of all!"

Abby's mother couldn't stop laughing. "I don't think you'll *ever* be able to make up your mind!"

The girls took turns posing next to and underneath the sculpture as Abby's aunts had done, so many years earlier. "I'm glad we can touch and climb this bear, but I see what you mean about fingerprints and oils left on the stone," Abby said.

"Probably every child who has ever walked by this sculpture over the past forty years has stopped to touch it. You can see that the face is well-worn and etched with oil and dust. If you look at the photo, you'll also see that the bear was a lot lighter forty years ago. But I have a feeling this is one sculpture Marshall Fredericks likes knowing children are allowed to touch and share."

That night, Abby and Kim chatted on the phone about each sculpture they had seen and made plans for the following weekend. Abby fell asleep writing in her journal.

Abby's journal: *There is a mysterious garden across from Quarton Lake. . . .*

Cranbrook

"Wake up, sleepyheads," Abby's mother called, "we're going to Cranbrook today."

Kim had slept over *again* and, like the previous week, the girls were slow to move in the morning.

"What's at Cranbrook?" Abby asked, rubbing her eyes.

"More sculptures, I bet," Kim said.

"Wait and see," Abby's mother teased, "and dress warmly. We're going to be outside all morning."

Cranbrook, located in Bloomfield Hills, is a community of art and architecture, science and art museums, independent schools, and an art academy. Some of the world's foremost twentieth-century artists helped design the buildings and furnishings as well as the layout of the campus. The community is a favorite destination for tourists and neighbors alike. Abby and Kim had visited the Cranbrook museums and played on the grounds since they were toddlers.

"Marshall Fredericks taught at Cranbrook and Kingswood schools in the 1930s,"

Abby's mom explained during the short drive to the campus. "He left a legacy of sculpture at the Cranbrook Academy of Art, the Science Museum, the girls' and boys' schools, and even at the outdoor theater."

"Mom," asked Abby, "did Marshall Fredericks design the fountain?" Abby had always been impressed by the grand appearance of the *Orpheus Fountain* and the reflecting pool that flanked the entrance to the Academy of Art Museum.

"No, the fountain was created by Carl Milles, who was Marshall Fredericks's teacher. In fact, it was Carl Milles who invited Marshall Fredericks to work and teach at Cranbrook, in 1932. I'm not surprised that you noticed some similarity in their work. Let's stop first at the Academy of Art so you can see the fountain. If you look carefully, you'll also see some Marshall Fredericks sculptures nearby."

"This chimpanzee, is it by Marshall Fredericks?" Kim asked as they bounded up the stairs of the Art Academy. Abby folded her arms and made a face mimicking the sculpture. Kim sat down mimicking Abby.

"It's called *The Thinker*," Abby's mother answered as she took a photograph. "You're getting very good at recognizing his work. Do you see anything else from here that Fredericks might have created?"

The girls looked around, but they didn't look down. Abby's mother had to point out what looked like a granite birdbath, called *Moray Eel with Fish*. "That looks creepy," Kim said.

Inside the Academy of Art Museum, Abby's mother showed the girls a small bronze statue called the *Bacchante*. "Next we're going to the Greek Theater. Bundle up, 'cause it's a bit of a hike from here," Abby's mother warned.

"This looks like a big version of the sculpture we just saw at the museum. What's this called?" Abby asked, looking at the solitary kneeling figure in the center of the empty reflecting pool.

"This is *Persephone*, the goddess of spring." Abby's mother explained. "And you're right. She's a life-size version of the *Bacchante*."

"How can there be two of the same sculpture?" Kim asked.

"Sculpture is different from a painting or a drawing. Sculptures can be made in different sizes, different patinas, and even different materials. I hope you'll understand how and why by the end of the day, but first I want you to

see one more Marshall Fredericks on the campus," Abby's mother explained. "It's called the *Two Sisters*."

"Is this it?" Kim asked. She was looking at a sculpture of two girls sitting on a park bench in one of the courtyards of the girls' school. "They don't look like his other figures."

"You're right, they're not by Marshall Fredericks. Cranbrook celebrates the creativity of some of the world's finest artists. Many different artists are responsible for the beauty of this place. Keep looking around. I'm sure you'll recognize them when you see them," Abby's mother said.

"Here they are," Abby called, as they meandered around the grounds. The *Two Sisters* centered a fountain in a rear courtyard.

"It should be called 'Big Sister, Little Sister,'" Kim said.

"I think it's also called *Mother and Child*," said Abby's mom.

"Then it could be us!" exclaimed Abby.

"Well, maybe," said her mother. "There are lots more Fredericks sculptures at Cranbrook, but it's really time for us to go, girls. You'll have more to find the next time you're here."

"Why do we have to go so soon?" implored Abby. "If there are more sculptures, why can't we just stay here longer?"

"I have a special surprise for you. I called Marshall Fredericks's studio the other day, and we've been invited to come and visit with his assistant before lunch. You both seemed to be having so much fun I almost lost track of the time."

"Is it too late to go to his studio?" asked Kim.

"Well, it's only a few miles south of here, in Royal Oak. I think we can get there in time."

31

The Royal Oak Studio

Carefully checking the addresses on busy Woodward Avenue, even Abby's mother was surprised when she eventually found the ivy-covered and well-hidden building. "You'd never know what creations exist inside this studio by the looks of the outside," she laughed. The three of them rang the doorbell and were greeted by a young woman.

"Hi, I'm Molly, one of Mr. Fredericks's assistants. If you girls would like to come inside, Mr. Fredericks said I could show you around."

Abby took Kim's hand, and they entered the cramped, daylight-lit, warehouse-type space. The studio was filled with plaster and bronze sculptures, certificates, plaques, photos, and medals—they covered the walls of each room and crowded every nook and cranny. There was very little space that wasn't occupied by a piece of art.

"Not many people can fit in here," Molly was saying, "but this is where Mr. Fredericks works." Abby and Kim followed Molly around as she pointed to various plaster models, small bronzes, clay forms, and mementoes. They bubbled with excitement and questions but, oddly, they both kept quiet during the tour. "Would you like to see how a sculpture is cast in bronze?" Molly asked.

Abby still held Kim's hand. They looked at each other and nodded their heads in unison as they followed the scent of wet clay and plaster into the sculpting area.

"Well, how do you think Mr. Fredericks would begin?" Molly asked.

"I guess with a drawing or sketch," Abby answered.

"Or maybe he makes something in clay?" asked Kim.

"You're both on the right track," Molly replied. "Mr. Fredericks sketches a picture first and then he makes a small clay model."

"But then how does it become so big?" asked Kim.

"Actually, a sculpture can be any size. Mr. Fredericks just starts with a small model and then he can decide how large he wants that particular sculpture to be." Molly pointed to a very small plaster model.

"Oh, I know that one," Abby said, "that's the *Leaping Gazelle*. We saw it last week on Belle Isle. But it was a lot larger, and it was in bronze."

"Exactly. Before sending a sculpture to the foundry to be cast in bronze, Mr. Fredericks makes a plaster model that's exactly the size and shape he wants. To do that, he first needs to build a skeleton-like support out of wood or metal. Here, look at this."

The girls looked at a large wooden form. It certainly didn't resemble any sculptures they had seen.

"This is called an armature," Molly explained. "Mr. Fredericks covers the armature with a thin layer of clay and shapes it until it looks exactly like his original design. And then things get really messy! That's where I can help. Look over here."

The girls turned to look at a plaster form cut into sections with bits of fabric and pipes sticking out of it. It barely resembled the original model sitting next to it.

"What's all that sticking out of the plaster?" Kim asked.

"We've added burlap to strengthen the plaster. And those are pipes."

"Pipes?" asked Abby. "What are the pipes for?"

"The pipes are used later to separate the plaster sections from the clay. It's amazing what kinds of material an artist uses," Molly laughed.

"But now you can hardly see the sculpture," Abby said. "I still don't understand how it will become bronze."

"This is only the first step in making a positive plaster model," Molly said patiently. "When we separate these plaster sections, using the pipes to help pull them from the clay, we then have the parts of a negative mold."

"Why a negative mold?" asked Kim.

"Think of a gelatin mold," continued Molly, "the form you pour the liquid into is the negative mold."

"Oh, I get it!" exclaimed Abby. "You pour the bronze into the negative mold. When you unmold it, you have the perfect shape you wanted."

"Well, we're not quite ready for the molten bronze yet," Molly laughed. "We use the negative mold to make a plaster model for the foundry."

"So plaster goes into the negative mold?" asked Kim.

"Yes," Molly answered, "but plaster will stick to plaster, so we have to shellac the inside of the negative mold. Then we add a separating agent called stearine."

"What's a separating agent?" asked Abby.

"Think back to the kitchen," Molly continued. "When you don't want something to stick when you're cooking, what do you do?"

"You grease the pan," piped in Kim.

"You have the right idea," Molly smiled. "We don't want the plaster from the negative mold to stick to the plaster of the positive model, so that's exactly what the

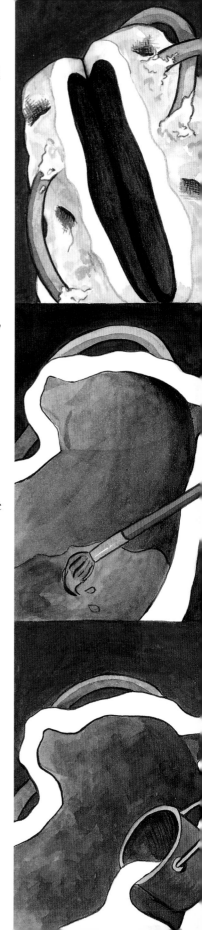

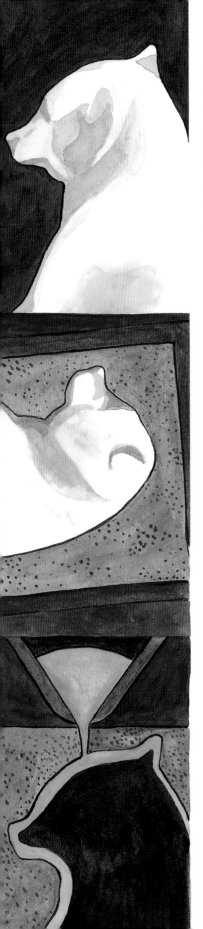

stearine does. In fact, I think it's even made out of beef tallow or fat, so it works just like grease in a pan. After the stearine is applied, we make the positive model in plaster. Just like before, we build up several layers of plaster inside the mold, but this time the pipes and burlap are very carefully hidden inside the layers of plaster. That way the plaster is strong but the model is hollow. When it's separated from the mold, the positive model will look like a perfect replica of the original clay model. That's what all these are in the studio," Molly continued to explain patiently, as she pointed around the room to several original plaster models.

"Now do you cover the models with bronze?" Abby asked.

"Not yet," Molly smiled. "The positive model is ready to be sent to the foundry, and that's where the bronze sculpture will take form." Molly motioned for the girls to sit, and she took out some photos to explain the work at the foundry. "The foundry will make their own molds with very special, finely packed French sand. When it's baked, the sand solidifies and takes on every single detail of the positive model."

"I get it! That becomes a negative sand mold. Now you pour the bronze into the sand mold?" asked Abby again.

"Almost," Molly continued explaining, "but because a large bronze would be too heavy if it were solid, the foundry also builds an inner core. Molten bronze is poured between the sand mold and that inner core. That way the finished bronze sculpture will be less than a half-inch thick."

"And that's it?" asked Kim.

Molly pointed to another photograph. "This is what a sculpture looks like after it is cast in bronze." There were seams where the sections had been welded together, and bronze rods were sticking out. "The foundry will grind away the rods and file down the rough edges," Molly explained, "and then Mr. Fredericks will decide what patina or finish the sculpture will have." Molly pointed to three sculptures on a table. "Look at those *Friendly Frogs* with three different patinas."

"I like the verdigris patina," said Abby. "That's the color of *The Spirit of Detroit* and the sculptures I saw from Quarton Lake."

"I like this golden color," said Kim. "That's the color of the boy at Northland and of the mouse at Eastland."

"That's gilded bronze," Molly said, "it has a layer of gold over the bronze."

"Wow! I can't believe how many steps it takes," sighed Kim. "Now I understand why there can be more than one of the same sculpture."

"Yes. Mr. Fredericks can reuse the same model or even enlarge it to any size he wants by making a new model." Molly pointed back to the cute little frogs on the table. "If you get a chance to see the Frederik Meijer Gardens and Sculpture Park in Grand Rapids, you'll find a *Friendly Frog* standing taller than you, as well as large sculptures of many of the models you see here."

"I've heard the sculpture gardens are spectacular in the summer, but I've never been there," Abby's mother said. "Perhaps we can plan a family trip there this summer." Then she looked at her watch. "Girls, please thank Molly. She's given us an amazing tour. We still haven't had lunch, and I've planned one more stop today."

Abby and Kim thanked their new friend Molly and reluctantly turned to leave. "Where are we going?" Abby asked.

"How about lunch at the zoo?" Abby's mother asked.

Detroit Zoological Park

The zoo was only minutes away from the studio. The girls ran to the depot, forgetting that the zoo train doesn't run in the winter. "Look," Kim pointed at a sculpture flanking the frozen pond by the station, "we just saw those birds at the studio." The girls stopped to take photos of the *Flying Wild Geese*, perched among the rocks, while Abby's mother caught up with them.

The sun was shining and the girls took off once again. The yellow-painted elephant tracks that lead the way around the zoo were barely visible on the freshly shoveled path. Few people were visiting the zoo that day. The girls' giggling echoed through the park as they chased each other along the path. Abby was the first to reach the Reptile House and see the *Flying Pterodactyls*.

"I remember these, Mom," Abby called back to her, "but I didn't know they were made by Marshall Fredericks."

"The *Flying Wild Geese* you just saw by the train station were installed a few years ago, but I grew up with the *Flying Pterodactyls*," Abby's mother said. "Look how you can see something different from each angle." She suggested that the girls photograph the sculpture from all four sides.

"I like these prehistoric dinosaurs a lot more than real crocodiles, lizards, and snakes—yech!" declared Kim.

Famished, they stopped inside a refreshment stand for lunch. This was the first time either girl had visited the zoo without seeing any live animals. But before they left, Abby's mom suggested they stop and see the polar bears. Surprisingly, the bears were a lot more lively and playful in the chill of the winter. They reminded Abby of the Quarton School bears.

"I loved today," said Abby, "but I'm really tired. Can we do this again some other time?"

"We'll see," said her mother. "It has been quite a day."

That night, snuggling under the covers, Abby stayed up recalling the day's events and writing in her journal.

Abby's journal: *What a great day. . . . We went to Cranbrook and Mr. Fredericks's studio. . . .*

The Detour

Winter vacation finally arrived. The car was packed and the skis were stowed for a trip up north. They left early in the morning, and Abby dozed, waking up only as the car was ascending the Zilwaukee Bridge. "We're going to take a little detour, Abby," her father said. "You're awake just in time!" He took an exit at the end of the bridge. "Your mother and I have been planning this special surprise for you." A few minutes later they arrived at the entrance to the campus of Saginaw Valley State University. Her father parked near a sign pointing toward the Arbury Fine Arts Center. "Let's go," her father said, opening the door.

As they approached the building, there was indeed a surprise. A life-size sculpture greeted Abby. "The *Two Bears*!" Abby exclaimed. "Look, they're humongous!" She ran up to the sculpture and climbed on the mother bear's lap. Looking around, her eyes rested on three oversized clowns lined up at the entrance to the center: *Juggler Clown*, *Acrobat Clown*, and the *Lovesick Clown*, who had an arrow piercing his heart.

"Mom, those clowns. . . . I saw small models of them at Mr. Fredericks's studio."

Abby caught sight of the *Pterodactyls* she had seen earlier at the zoo. She ran ahead without waiting for her parents, but they trailed closely behind, not wanting to miss the look on her face the moment she entered the Marshall M. Fredericks Sculpture Museum.

Inside was a two-storied room of light and wonder, filled from floor to ceiling with the original white plaster models for hundreds of Marshall Fredericks's sculptures. For a moment, Abby stood in silence. The soft indirect light lent a glow to the room and all the sculptures within. The room was magical.

"Mom, Dad, I can't believe this," Abby whispered in awe. She took her father's hand and led him through the gallery, her heart dancing. Abby recognized many of the sculptures she had seen in the last few weeks. To her amazement, there were just as many new ones. She twirled herself around,

taking in the scope of the museum, her eyes returning to the graceful gazelle she remembered from the fountain on Belle Isle. By now Abby was sure of her uncontested, favorite sculpture but she didn't tell her mom.

"It's incredible seeing so many works all in one place," Abby's mother said, putting her arm around Abby's shoulders and hugging her. The three of them walked around the room together. "These are the original models for sculptures created throughout Mr. Fredericks's career. What a fantastic collection together in one space. We'd have to travel all over the world to see all of them."

"All over the world?" inquired Abby. "Do people know Marshall Fredericks outside of Michigan?"

"Oh, honey," Abby's mother smiled gently, "he's not just our little secret. Mr. Fredericks's sculptures are enjoyed throughout the world, in places as far away as Japan, Sweden, and Denmark. It's because he has been living and creating in our community for more than sixty years that this corner of Michigan is like an outdoor museum of his life's work.

"Maybe you were right when you said Marshall Fredericks was in charge of decorating the city!" Abby laughed.

Abby's journal: *Mom and Dad took me to the most special place today. . . . I didn't have my camera with me, but they bought me some postcards. . . .*

The Skating Party

Abby's birthday was approaching as the end of January neared. She had decided to have a skating party and share the secret of Quarton Lake with the rest of her friends. The day of her party was cold, crisp, and bright, and there were lots of people on the ice. A group of boys Abby knew were playing hockey across the lake. They had set up their goals very near her secret space. The girls tried to catch a glimpse of the hidden treasures Abby pointed to, at a spot across the ice, but the boys' game was in the way. They skated close to the hockey players, not realizing they were invading the playing field.

"Hey, Abby, what gives? You have to move," cried one of the boys. "You're in the middle of our game!"

"Can't you guys play over there?" Abby asked. "I want to show my friends the mystery of Quarton Lake."

The boys stopped playing and skated over to the group of girls. "What mystery?" one of them asked.

"Look through those trees," Abby replied. "Do you see those sculptures? That's the house of my favorite artist, Marshall Fredericks. He's really famous, and did you know his kids even went to our school?"

The children peered through the trees. A fresh snow had fallen, and the verdigris-patinated sculptures stood proudly, silhouetted against the glistening snow.

"Oh, wow," said one of the boys, "there's that really cool eagle downtown."

"I've seen those geese before," called one of the girls. "They're at the zoo!"

"Oh, look," another boy said. "I've seen that deer before."

"That's the *Leaping Gazelle*," Abby told him, proud that all her friends and classmates were so intrigued by her discovery.

"How do you know so much about those sculptures, Abby? They're really cool."

Abby stood tall. "Oh, they're all around town," she said knowingly. "I'll bring my journal to school Monday to show you some of my favorites—ones like *The Spirit of Detroit*. . . ."

One of the boys interrupted her. "Hey, Abby, isn't that the big green guy who wore the Red Wings jersey when the Wings won the Stanley Cup? My dad took a picture of me in front of it, but I didn't know who the sculptor was. That is awesome."

Abby was so delighted by their response that she invited the boys to share her birthday cake. It was a wonderful party.

"We have one stop to make before we go home," Abby's mom told her as the last of the kids left the party. Abby pulled off her skates and climbed into the car. Her father drove across the bridge and around to the other side of Quarton Lake, stopping in front of a building that resembled a small French chateau. Fresh snow draped the entrance, making the house look like it belonged in a fairy tale. There was no doorbell.

"Knock," Abby's father encouraged.

Abby grabbed the large black door knocker and knocked three times. A tall and regal white-haired gentleman opened the door and greeted Abby with a warm smile.

"Come in, I've been expecting you," the gentleman said, with a twinkle in his eye.

Abby couldn't believe it. She was standing face-to-face with Mr. Fredericks, the real artist! He looked even taller than in the photographs she had seen of him at the sculpture museum.

"Follow me," Mr. Fredericks said, as he took her by the hand and led her into the kitchen, where his wife was waiting.

"You must be Abigail," Mrs. Fredericks said, as she motioned for Abby and her parents to sit. "We've heard a lot about you—and we've heard it is your birthday!" Abby and her family sat around the Frederickses' kitchen table, warming up with hot chocolate and cookies. Her parents chatted with the Frederickses but Abby was momentarily speechless.

Mrs. Fredericks winked at her husband as he ceremoniously put his hand into his pocket and withdrew a tiny package, placing it in Abby's hand. "Happy Birthday, Abigail."

Abby put down her mug to unwrap the tiny package. "The *Gazelle*!" she cried, staring at a little silver pin. "How could you have known?" Tears welled up in her eyes. "Thank you, Mr. Fredericks, this is the nicest present ever!" She looked into the artist's eyes, as he gently took the gazelle from her hands and pinned it onto her sweater. "Is that one of your favorites too?" she asked.

"I like them all, Abby, but the *Gazelle* reminds me of you."

Abby beamed and stretched her neck as if she were indeed the doe-like animal. Giddy with happiness and bursting with excitement, she began to rattle off the names of some of the sculptures that had captivated her. She told Mr. Fredericks about the journal she was keeping to keep track of her discoveries, and about the trips she had taken to Detroit and around the state in search of his sculptures. "But really the best part," she confided, "was the mystery at Quarton Lake!"

"Abigail, you have made an old man very happy. As much as I've always enjoyed creating sculptures that would inspire people, I've always had a special place in my heart for children. It gives me such great pleasure to see a child smile at one of my baboons or bears, and I'm so honored that you enjoy my work. I remember how much fun my own children used to have climbing and playing on *The Boy and Bear* when they were little. That's the joy I felt creating it, and what I want people to feel when they see a sculpture. I do hope you'll find the same delight and inspiration in my work when you're an adult and I am long gone. *That* has been my life's goal."

Abby's mother began to speak. "Abby, we've taken a lot of the Frederickses' time. . . ."

Abby glanced up at Mr. Fredericks. "May I see your backyard?" she asked boldly.

Mr. Fredericks laughed as he put his arm around her shoulders and led her through two French doors out into his yard. "This is a special place, and I put these sculptures here for my own children. They always seemed to enjoy being around them," he said, as he walked alongside Abby into the snow-covered garden. "But I must confess, I think they make *me* happy too," he said with a chuckle.

Abby was enchanted. Dozens of sculptures decorated the walls and grounds, some facing the lake, others hidden around bends in the garden. Wherever she turned she met with another surprise: saintly figures stood as sentinels overlooking the garden, a queue of animals watched over a family of baboons, *The Lion and Mouse* played by the door, a duckling announced a stairway, eagles and seagulls stood silhouetted against the lake. Abby loved every sculpture, even the ones she had never seen before. To her, they were all like old friends.

Mr. Fredericks in his studio, next to the *Leaping Gazelle* and surrounded by plaster models and bronzes, 1989

Mr. Fredericks working with wet plaster to create a model, 1952

Mr. Fredericks working on the scale model for the monumental Veterans Memorial *Victory Eagle*, 1946

MARSHALL M. FREDERICKS (1908–1998)

Marshall M. Fredericks was born in Rock Island, Illinois, in 1908. He grew up in Cleveland, Ohio, and graduated in 1930 from the Cleveland School of Art. That year, Mr. Fredericks was awarded a traveling fellowship and chose to study in Sweden with the famed sculptor Carl Milles (1875––1955). Milles's monumental sculptures were the early inspiration for Mr. Fredericks's desire to create large, public sculptures. In 1932, Mr. Fredericks followed Milles, who had become his mentor, to the Cranbrook Academy of Art, in Bloomfield Hills, Michigan, where Milles was then artist-in-residence.

Other than his service in the Army Corps of Engineers, and later the Army Air Corps, during World War II, Mr. Fredericks resided in Michigan for more than sixty years. He taught sculpture at Cranbrook from 1932–1942, and after returning from the war, he established his working studio in Royal Oak. There, in a tightly packed and cramped space, he created many of the enormous figurative sculptures that grace public sites throughout the world, working right up to his death in 1998.

Mr. Fredericks and his wife Rosalind had five children. He especially loved young people, and many of his works, especially his animals, are designed to enchant them. His sculptures and monuments have often become the icon for a community or organization—such as *The Spirit of Detroit*, which is the symbol of that city. Mr. Fredericks often donated his artistic fee so that communities could afford his sculptures.

The large concentration of his public sculptures in Michigan, especially in the Detroit area, is due to his long-standing presence in the community as well as his philanthropy. As the beneficiary of his legacy, Michigan luckily maintains its role as an outdoor museum of his work.

THE SCULPTURES IN
MARSHALL FREDERICKS'S STUDIO

Note: Although some sculptures in public collections may be called by other names, all references in this book adhere to the documented titles from the Marshall Fredericks Studio.

1. *Friendly Frog*
2. *Rabbit*
3. *Baboon with Baby Chimpanzee*
4. *Don Quixote de la Mancha*
5. *Hawk*
6. *Grouse*
7. *Ugly Duckling*
8. *Baboon and Sleeping Child*
9. *The Thinker*
10. *Two Bears*
11. *Anniversary Baboons*
12. *Victory Eagle*
13. *The Spirit of Detroit*
14. *American Eagle*
15. *Wild Swan from Indian and Wild Swans*
16. *Temptation*
17. *Warrior Saint*
18. *Eve/Knowledge of Good and Evil*
19. *The Guests Have Arrived*
20. *Indian Rider*
21. *Pony Express Rider*
22. *Indian and Bears*
23. *Indian, Deer and Wolves*
24. *Lovesick Clown*
25. *Freedom of the Human Spirit*
26. *Siberian Ram*
27. *Fish Kingdom*
28. *Sketch Model for Celestial Fountain*
29. *Acrobat Clown*
30. *Juggler Clown*
31. *The Boy and Bear*
32. *Day*
33. *Persephone*
34. *Female Baboon*
35. *Male Baboon*
36. *Leaping Gazelle*

Scenes from Detroit during the 1950s, bottom of pages 14–15 from left to right:

Victory Eagle on facade of the Veterans Memorial Building, *Reliefs* on the Horace H. Rackham Educational Memorial Building, Play Furniture from the Holden Great Ape Exhibit at the Detroit Zoological Park, Textile Industry *Relief* from the Ford Rotunda, A *Harlequin* from the Henry and Edsel Ford Auditorium

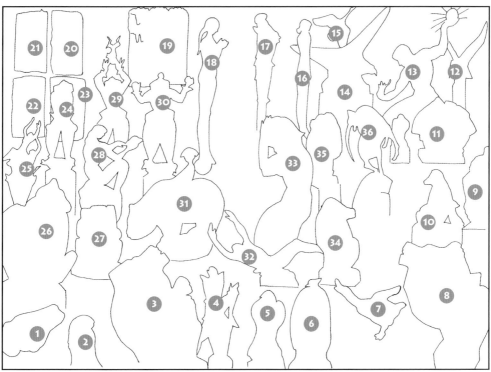

SELECTED MARSHALL FREDERICKS SCULPTURES IN MICHIGAN AND AROUND THE GREAT LAKES*

MICHIGAN

Albion

Floyd Starr–Starr Commonwealth
The Princess and the Unicorn–Brueckner Museum, Starr Commonwealth

Alma

**American Eagle*–Alma College
Flying Wild Geese–Alma College

Ann Arbor

Adventurer, Aesop's Fables, Hiawatha, Musicians, Naturalist, Scientist, Student Motif, Baboons symbolizing Music and Science, and 29 untitled reliefs representing God, nature and man–Literature, Science and Arts Building, University of Michigan
**American Eagle*–University of Michigan Stadium
Arthur H. Vandenberg–Rackham Memorial Building, University of Michigan
Dream of the Young Girl, Dream of the Young Man–East Facade, Literature, Science and Arts Building, University of Michigan

Birmingham

+***American Eagle*–First Presbyterian Church of Birmingham
Flying Wild Geese–Greenwood Cemetery
Flying Wild Geese Medallion–First Presbyterian Church of Birmingham

+*The Fountain of Eternal Life*–Victor Saroki and Associates
Freedom of the Human Spirit–Shain Park
Guardian Angel–St. James Episcopal Church
Veterans Memorial, Birmingham City Hall
The Guests Have Arrived (named *Student Body* by students)–Birmingham Pierce Elementary School
+*Hiawatha*–Birmingham Covington School
Leaping Gazelle–Grave of Marshall M. Fredericks, Greenwood Cemetery
Siberian Ram–Baldwin Public Library
+*Two Bears* (or *Friends, Big and Small*, named by students)–Birmingham Quarton Elementary School
+*Wings of the Morning*–First Presbyterian Church of Birmingham
Young Knight–Birmingham Seaholm High School

Bloomfield Hills

Baboon of the Theater, Playing a Ham–St. Dunstan's Theater at Cranbrook
+*Bacchante* or *Persephone*–Cranbrook Art Museum
+*The Boy and Bear*–George P. Way Elementary School
+*Central Figure* from *Fountain of Eternal Life*–Kirk in the Hills
Childhood Friends–Cranbrook Academy of Art
Christ and the Children–St. Hugo of the Hills

---

* Special arrangements should be made before visiting the interiors of churches and schools. Also note that museum collections are often enormous. Usually only a portion of a collection is on display, with the rest in storage. It is advisable to call the museum's curator in advance if there are particular sculptures you wish to see.

+ Marshall Fredericks made smaller versions, which he called scale models, of his monumental sculptures. These smaller versions might be half-scale, quarter-scale, or even smaller maquettes (small studies or sketches for larger works). They are frequently found in schools, libraries, and private collections. A + in front of a title indicates that sculpture is a scale model.

**The documented names for the *Victory Eagle* and *American Eagle* are inconsistent. The names given here refer to the sculptures identified on page 56.

+*Circus Clown*–Brookside School, Cranbrook
Fish, Frog and Lizard Fountain–Thornlea, Cranbrook
George Gough Booth and Ellen Scripps Booth–Cranbrook Institute of Science
Henry Booth–Brookside School, Cranbrook
Medallion–Kingswood School, Cranbrook
Moray Eel and Fish–Cranbrook Art Museum
Persephone or *Bacchante*–Greek Theater, Cranbrook
+*Two Sisters*–Cranbrook Academy of Art
The Thinker–Cranbrook Art Museum
Torso of a Dancer–Cranbrook Art Museum
+*Two Bears*–Fox Hills Pre-School, Bloomfield Hills Public Schools
Two Sisters or *Mother and Child*–Kingswood School, Cranbrook
William Oliver Stevens–Cranbrook Academy of Art
Wings of the Morning–Kirk in the Hills

Clawson

+****Victory Eagle*–Sterling Bank

Commerce

Flying Wild Geese–Huron Valley Sinai Hospital

Dearborn

Henry Ford Memorial: Childhood, Ford Empire, Formative Years, Ford Cars, Henry Ford–Henry Ford Centennial Library
Mercury–Research Center, Henry Ford Museum Collection
+*Siberian Ram*–Fairlane Garden

Detroit

Alexander Blain Senior, Alexander Blain, M.D.F.A.C.S.–Detroit Historical Museum
Automotive Engineering, Chinese Astronomer, Education and Science, Knowledge, Learning, Pegasus, Primitive Education, Steelworkers, and 28 untitled reliefs–Horace H. Rackham Educational Memorial Building
Circus Parade–Henry and Edsel Ford Auditorium (currently closed to the public)
Edwin Denby Memorial–Denby Technical and Preparatory High School
Eve–The Detroit Institute of Arts
Family and Justice Plaques (4)–Coleman A. Young Municipal Center (formerly City-County Building), courtrooms
Flying Wild Geese–Elmwood Cemetery

Ford Empire–Henry and Edsel Ford Auditorium (currently closed to the public)
Great Seal of the United States–UAW-Ford National Programs Center (formerly Veterans Memorial Building)
Harlequins–Henry and Edsel Ford Auditorium (currently closed to the public)
Jerome P. Cavanaugh–The Detroit Institute of Arts
Leaping Gazelle–First Federal of Michigan
Levi L. Barbour Memorial Fountain: Leaping Gazelle with *Grouse, Hawk, Otter,* and *Rabbit*–Belle Isle Park
Mary A. Rackham–Engineering Society, Horace H. Rackham Educational Memorial Building
Mary Soper Pope Memorial Award Medals (3)–The Detroit Institute of Arts
Michigan Academy of Science, Arts and Letters Medallion–Detroit Historical Museum
Michigan Society of Architects Medallion–Detroit Historical Museum
Pylons (7): *Battle of the Great Lakes, Civil War, Founding of Detroit, Indian Wars, Spanish-American War, World War I, World War II*–UAW-Ford National Programs Center (formerly Veterans Memorial Building)
Seal of the City of Detroit–Coleman A. Young Municipal Center (formerly City-County Building)
Seal of the City of Detroit–Detroit Historical Museum
Seal of Wayne Country–Coleman A. Young Municipal Center (formerly City-County Building)
Seal of Wayne Country–Detroit Historical Museum
Siberian Ram–Renaissance Center People Mover Station
The Spirit of Detroit–Coleman A. Young Municipal Center (formerly City-County Building)
Tracy W. McGregor–McGregor Elementary School
Tracy W. McGregor–McGregor Memorial Conference Center, Wayne State University
****Victory Eagle*–UAW-Ford National Programs Center (formerly Veterans Memorial Building)

Farmington

Cross–Our Lady of Sorrows

Ferndale

+*Two Bears*–Ferndale Public Library

Flint

Friendly Frog–Flint Children's Museum

Grand Haven

Flying Gulls Fountain–Courtyard between the Loutit District Library and the Grand Haven Community Center

Grand Rapids

Acrobat Clown, Juggler Clown, and *Lovesick Clown*–Frederik Meijer Gardens and Sculpture Park

**American Eagle–Frederik Meijer Gardens and Sculpture Park

Baboon and Friend–Frederik Meijer Gardens and Sculpture Park

Baboon and Sleeping Child–Frederik Meijer Gardens and Sculpture Park

Baboon with Baby Chimpanzee–Frederik Meijer Gardens and Sculpture Park

The Boy and Bear–Frederik Meijer Gardens and Sculpture Park

Don Quixote de la Mancha–Meijer Inc. Headquarters

Flying Wild Geese–Frederik Meijer Gardens and Sculpture Park

Flying Wild Geese–Van Andel Museum Center of the Public Museum of Grand Rapids

Friendly Dragons (2)–Frederik Meijer Gardens and Sculpture Park

Friendly Frog–Frederik Meijer Gardens and Sculpture Park

Grouse–Frederik Meijer Gardens and Sculpture Park

Hawk–Frederik Meijer Gardens and Sculpture Park

Leaping Gazelle–Frederik Meijer Gardens and Sculpture Park

Lord Byron–Frederik Meijer Gardens and Sculpture Park

+*Night and Day*–Frederik Meijer Gardens and Sculpture Park

Otter–Frederik Meijer Gardens and Sculpture Park

Rabbit–Frederik Meijer Gardens and Sculpture Park

+*Seven Saints and Sinners*–Frederik Meijer Gardens and Sculpture Park

Siberian Ram–Frederik Meijer Gardens and Sculpture Park

The Swan and the Ugly Duckling–Frederik Meijer Gardens and Sculpture Park

The Thinker–Frederik Meijer Gardens and Sculpture Park

Two Bears–Frederik Meijer Gardens and Sculpture Park

**Victory Eagle–Frederik Meijer Gardens and Sculpture Park

**Victory Eagle–John Ball Zoological Gardens

Wings of the Morning–Frederik Meijer Gardens and Sculpture Park

Young Knight–Ottawa Hills High School

Greenville

The Swan and the Ugly Duckling–Hans Christian Anderson Fountain, Heritage Park

Grosse Pointe

+*The Boy and Bear*–Grosse Pointe Public Library, Central Branch

Dexter M. Ferry, portrait relief–Dexter M. Ferry Elementary School

Flying Wild Geese–Christ Church Episcopal

George Mertz Slocum–Grosse Pointe Yacht Club

Peter Austin Whyte–St. John Hospital

Self-Portrait (named *Dexter* by students)–Dexter M. Ferry Elementary School

Harper Woods

The Lion and Mouse–Eastland Center

Indian River

Christ on the Cross–Cross in the Woods Parish

Interlochen

Alden B. Dow, Architect–Interlochen Center for the Arts

Two Bears–Interlochen Center for the Arts

Kalamazoo

Flying Wild Geese–Kellogg Foundation

Lansing

Seals of the Circuit Court of Ingham County (4)–Ingham County Circuit Court (in storage)

Mackinac Island

William Beaumont–Beaumont Memorial

Madison Heights

**+*American Eagle*–Madison High School

Marquette

Flying Wild Geese–Northern Michigan University

Midland

Alden B. Dow, Architect–Midland Center for the Arts

Anniversary Baboons–Alden B. Dow Home and Studio

+*Childhood Friends*–Alden B. Dow Home and Studio

Leaping Gazelle–Dow Gardens

+*Seven Saints and Sinners*–Alden B. Dow Home and Studio

Seven Saints and Sinners–Midland Center for the Arts

Mt. Clemens

John F. Kennedy–Macomb County Building

Muskegon

Leaping Gazelle–Muskegon Museum of Art

Pontiac

Chief Pontiac–30 North Saginaw

Head, Chief Pontiac–National City Bank, 44300 Woodward Avenue

Port Huron

Night and Day Fountain–McMorran Auditorium, McMorran Place

Sunburst Clock–McMorran Auditorium, McMorran Place

River Rouge

Ford Model "S"–U.S. Post Office

Rochester

Angel in the Hand of God–Crittenton Hospital

Seven Saints and Sinners Fountain–Kresge Library, Oakland University

Rochester Hills

The Swan and the Ugly Duckling–Hans Christian Anderson Fountain, Danish Village

Royal Oak

+*Acrobat Clown, Juggler Clown*, and *Lovesick Clown*–Royal Oak Public Library

Family, Protected by Healing Herbs–William Beaumont Hospital

Female Baboon and *Male Baboon*–Detroit Zoological Park

Flying Pterodactyls–Holden Museum of Living Reptiles, Detroit Zoological Park

Flying Wild Geese–Main Train Station, Detroit Zoological Park

Leaping Gazelle–Detroit Zoological Park

Mankind and Primates Relief–Detroit Zoological Park

Star Dream Fountain–Barbara Hallman Plaza, Civic Center

+*Two Bears*–Royal Oak Public Library

William Beaumont–William Beaumont Hospital

Saginaw

Flying Wild Geese–Lucille E. Andersen Memorial Garden, Andersen Enrichment Center

Flying Wild Geese–Saginaw Art Museum

Sault Ste. Marie

Walker Lee Cisler–Lake Superior State College

Southfield

The Boy and Bear–Northland Center

+*Leaping Gazelle*–Southfield City Hall

+*Two Bears*–Southfield Public Library

Sterling Heights

Two Bears–Sterling Heights Public Library

St. Joseph

Otter–Krasl Art Center

University Center, Saginaw Valley State University

200+ original plaster models, sculptures, jewelry, sketches, drawings and memorabilia–Marshall M. Fredericks Sculpture Museum

Outdoor Sculptures on campus:

Acrobat Clown, Juggler Clown, and *Lovesick Clown*–Arbury Fine Arts Center, South Entrance

The Boy and Bear–Sculpture Garden

Christ and the Children–Sculpture Garden

Don Quixote de la Mancha–Sculpture Garden

Female Baboon and *Male Baboon*–Arbury Fine Arts Center, North Entrance

Flying Pterodactyls–Arbury Fine Arts Center, North Entrance

+*Figure and Sphere* from *Fountain of Eternal Life*–Founders Hall

Leaping Gazelle Fountain–SVSU Quadrangle
The Lion and Mouse–Sculpture Garden
Night and Day Fountain–Sculpture Garden
Otter–Sculpture Garden
Persephone–Sculpture Garden
Siberian Ram–Sculpture Garden
Two Bears–Sculpture Garden
Two Sisters or *Mother and Child*–Sculpture Garden
Wings of the Morning–Sculpture Garden
Youth in the Hands of God–Garden Wall

Waterford

Christ the Good Shepherd–Central United Methodist Church

Wyandotte

Childhood Friends–Jefferson Elementary School

OTHER GREAT LAKES STATES

Illinois

Farm Animals–U.S. Post Office, Sandwich

Indiana

Christ and the Children–St. John's Lutheran Church, Fort Wayne

Ohio

Birth of Atomic Age Fountain–National Exchange Club, Toledo
Cleveland War Memorial: The Fountain of Eternal Life–Cleveland
Playing Bears Fountain–Camp Ho Mita Koda, Newbury
Industry and Employment, Motion in Nature and *Recreational Activities*, Reliefs–Ohio Bureau of Employment Services, Columbus
The Ohio Union Reliefs–Ohio Union, Ohio State University, Columbus
Transportation by Man–Department of Transportation Building, Columbus
***The Victory Eagle*–John Weld Peck Federal Building, Cincinnati

Wisconsin

Indian and Wild Swans–Milwaukee Public Museum

ALBUM PAGES

Sculpture _____

Location _____

Comments _____

_____

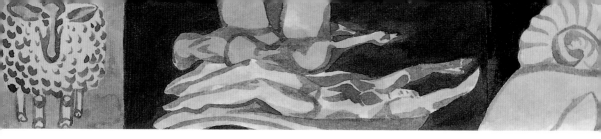

ALBUM PAGES

Sculpture _____

Location _____

Comments _____

_____

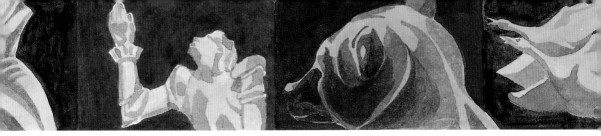

ALBUM PAGES

Sculpture _____

Location _____

Comments _____

_____

ALBUM PAGES

Sculpture _____

Location _____

Comments _____

_____

ALBUM PAGES

Sculpture _____

Location _____

Comments _____

_____

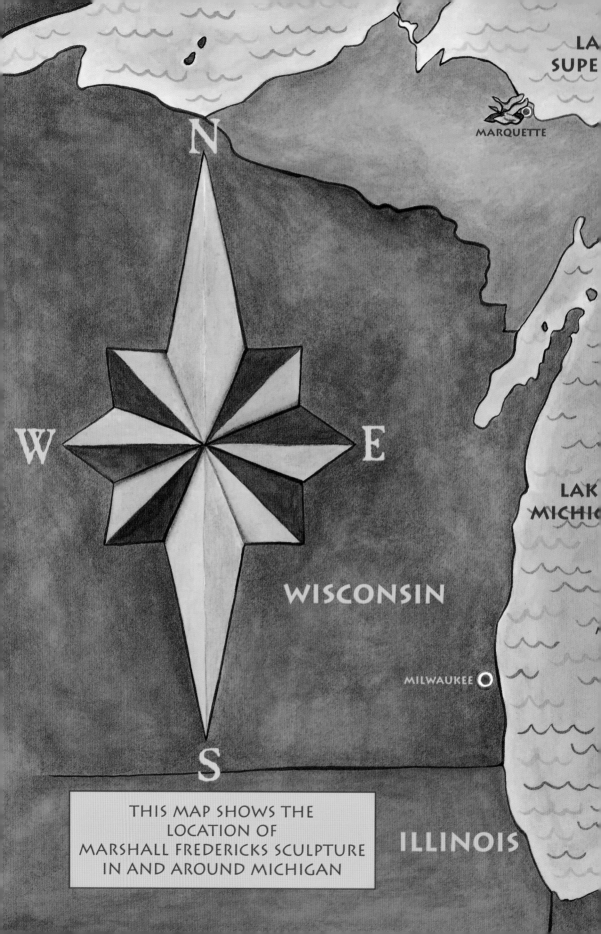

LA
SUPE

MARQUETTE

N

W   E

LAK
MICHIG

S

WISCONSIN

MILWAUKEE O

THIS MAP SHOWS THE
LOCATION OF
MARSHALL FREDERICKS SCULPTURE
IN AND AROUND MICHIGAN

ILLINOIS

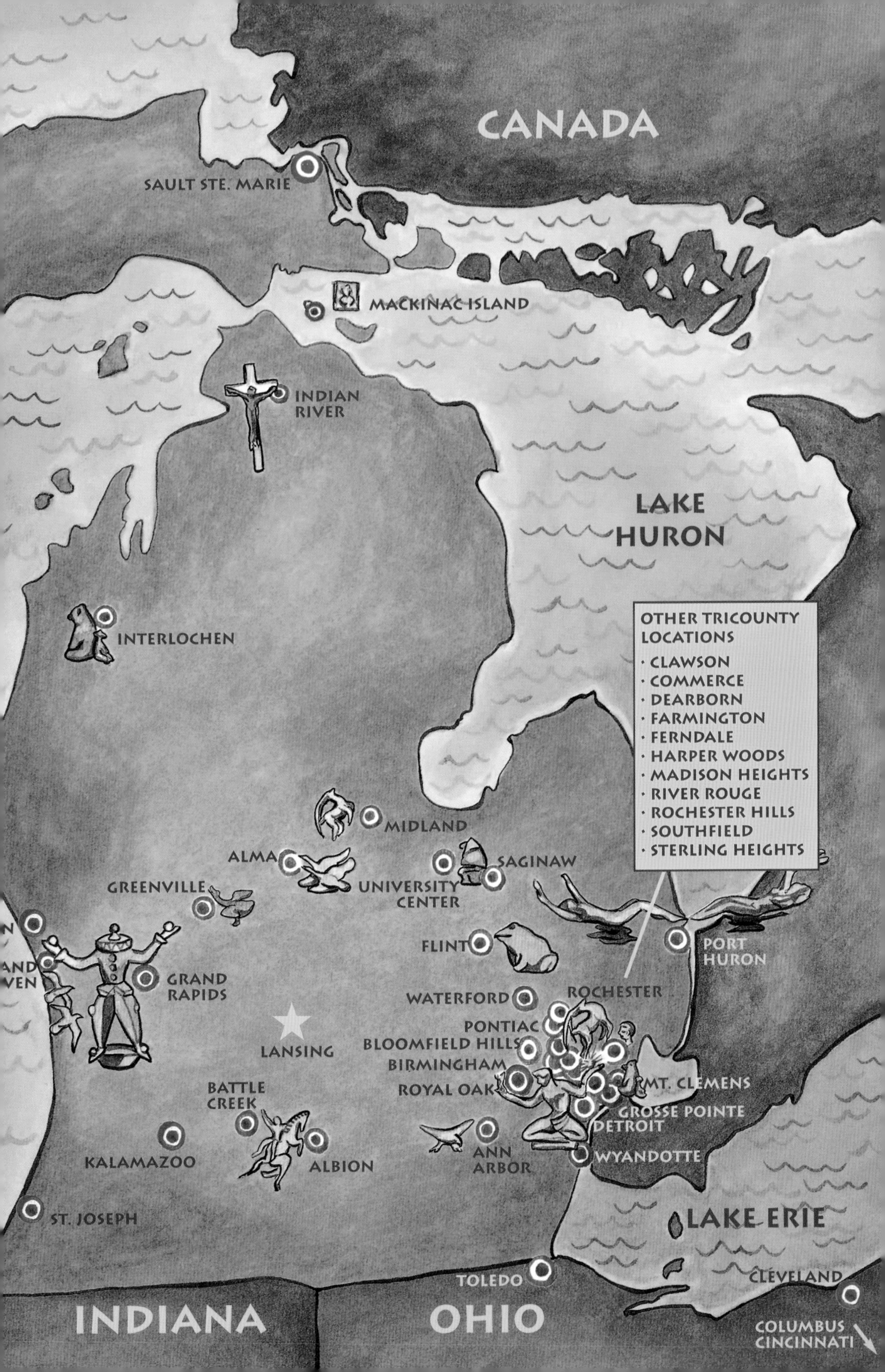

CANADA

SAULT STE. MARIE

MACKINAC ISLAND

INDIAN RIVER

LAKE HURON

INTERLOCHEN

MIDLAND

ALMA

SAGINAW

UNIVERSITY CENTER

GREENVILLE

AND VEN

FLINT

PORT HURON

GRAND RAPIDS

WATERFORD

ROCHESTER

LANSING

PONTIAC
BLOOMFIELD HILLS
BIRMINGHAM
ROYAL OAK

MT. CLEMENS

BATTLE CREEK

GROSSE POINTE
DETROIT

KALAMAZOO

ALBION

ANN ARBOR

WYANDOTTE

ST. JOSEPH

LAKE ERIE

TOLEDO

CLEVELAND

INDIANA

OHIO

COLUMBUS
CINCINNATI

TITLES IN THE
GREAT LAKES BOOKS SERIES

Lake Erie and Lake St. Clair Handbook, by Stanley J. Bolsenga and Charles E. Herndendorf, 1993

Queen of the Lakes, by Mark Thompson, 1994

Iron Fleet: The Great Lakes in World War II, by George J. Joachim, 1994

Turkey Stearnes and the Detroit Stars: The Negro Leagues in Detroit, 1919–1933, by Richard Bak, 1994

Pontiac and the Indian Uprising, by Howard H. Peckham, 1994 (reprint)

Charting the Inland Seas: A History of the U.S. Lake Survey, by Arthur M. Woodford, 1994 (reprint)

Ojibwa Narratives of Charles and Charlotte Kawbawgam and Jacques LePique, 1893–1895. Recorded with Notes by Homer H. Kidder, edited by Arthur P. Bourgeois, 1994, co-published with the Marquette County Historical Society

Strangers and Sojourners: A History of Michigan's Keweenaw Peninsula, by Arthur W. Thurner, 1994

Win Some, Lose Some: G. Mennen Williams and the New Democrats, by Helen Washburn Berthelot, 1995

Sarkis, by Gordon and Elizabeth Orear, 1995

The Northern Lights: Lighthouses of the Upper Great Lakes, by Charles K. Hyde, 1995 (reprint)

Kids Catalog of Michigan Adventures, second edition, by Ellyce Field, 1995

Rumrunning and the Roaring Twenties: Prohibition on the Michigan-Ontario Waterway, by Philip P. Mason, 1995

In the Wilderness with the Red Indians, by E. R. Baierlein, translated by Anita Z. Boldt, edited by Harold W. Moll, 1996

Elmwood Endures: History of a Detroit Cemetery, by Michael Franck, 1996

Master of Precision: Henry M. Leland, by Mrs. Wilfred C. Leland with Minnie Dubbs Millbrook, 1996 (reprint)

Haul-Out: New and Selected Poems, by Stephen Tudor, 1996

Kids Catalog of Michigan Adventures, third edition, by Ellyce Field, 1997

Beyond the Model T: The Other Ventures of Henry Ford, revised edition, by Ford R. Bryan, 1997

Young Henry Ford: A Picture History of the First Forty Years, by Sidney Olson, 1997 (reprint)

The Coast of Nowhere: Meditations on Rivers, Lakes and Streams, by Michael Delp, 1997

From Saginaw Valley to Tin Pan Alley: Saginaw's Contribution to American Popular Music, 1890–1955, by R. Grant Smith, 1998

The Long Winter Ends, by Newton G. Thomas, 1998 (reprint)

Bridging the River of Hatred: The Pioneering Efforts of Detroit Police Commissioner George Edwards, by Mary M. Stolberg, 1998

Toast of the Town: The Life and Times of Sunnie Wilson, by Sunnie Wilson with John Cohassey, 1998

These Men Have Seen Hard Service: The First Michigan Sharpshooters in the Civil War, by Raymond J. Herek, 1998

A Place for Summer: One Hundred Years at Michigan and Trumbull, by Richard Bak, 1998

Early Midwestern Travel Narratives: An Annotated Bibliography, 1634–1850, by Robert R. Hubach, 1998 (reprint)

All-American Anarchist: Joseph A. Labadie and the Labor Movement, by Carlotta R. Anderson, 1998

Michigan in the Novel, 1816–1996: An Annotated Bibliography, by Robert Beasecker, 1998

"Time by Moments Steals Away": The 1848 Journal of Ruth Douglass, by Robert L. Root, Jr., 1998

The Detroit Tigers: A Pictorial Celebration of the Greatest Players and Moments in Tigers' History, updated edition, by William M. Anderson, 1999

Father Abraham's Children: Michigan Episodes in the Civil War, by Frank B. Woodford, 1999 (reprint)

Letter from Washington, 1863–1865, by Lois Bryan Adams, edited and with an introduction by Evelyn Leasher, 1999

Wonderful Power: The Story of Ancient Copper Working in the Lake Superior Basin, by Susan R. Martin, 1999

A Sailor's Logbook: A Season aboard Great Lakes Freighters, by Mark L. Thompson, 1999

Huron: The Seasons of a Great Lake, by Napier Shelton, 1999

Tin Stackers: The History of the Pittsburgh Steamship Company, by Al Miller, 1999

Art in Detroit Public Places, revised edition, text by Dennis Nawrocki, photographs by David Clements, 1999

Brewed in Detroit: Breweries and Beers Since 1830, by Peter H. Blum, 1999

Detroit Kids Catalog: A Family Guide for the 21st Century, by Ellyce Field, 2000

"Expanding the Frontiers of Civil Rights": Michigan, 1948–1968, by Sidney Fine, 2000

Graveyard of the Lakes, by Mark L. Thompson, 2000

Enterprising Images: The Goodridge Brothers, African American Photographers, 1847–1922, by John Vincent Jezierski, 2000

The Sandstone Architecture of the Lake Superior Region, by Kathryn Bishop Eckert, 2000

Arab Detroit: From Margin to Mainstream, edited by Nabeel Abraham and Andrew Shryock, 2000

New Poems from the Third Coast: Contemporary Michigan Poetry, edited by Michael Delp, Conrad Hilberry, and Josie Kearns, 2000

Looking Beyond Race: The Life of Otis Milton Smith, by Otis Milton Smith and Mary M. Stolberg, 2000

Mail by the Pail, by Colin Bergel, illustrated by Mark Koenig, 2000

Great Lakes Journey: A New Look at America's Freshwater Coast, by William Ashworth, 2000

A Life in the Balance: The Memoirs of Stanley J. Winkelman, by Stanley J. Winkelman, 2000

Schooner Passage: Sailing Ships and the Lake Michigan Frontier, by Theodore J. Karamanski, 2000

The Outdoor Museum: The Magic of Michigan's Marshall M. Fredericks, by Marcy Heller Fisher, illustrated by Christine Collins Woomer, 2001